W9-BLJ-090

A GIFT FOR

FROM

DATE

POINT OF GRACE

when love came down
at christmas

With Luke V. Gibbs and Terri Gibbs

J. COUNTRYMAN

NASHVILLE, TENNESSEE

Published by J. Countryman, a division of Thomas Nelson, Inc,
Nashville, Tennessee 37214.

Project editor: Terri Gibbs

Designed by Uttley/DouPonce DesignWorks, Sisters, Oregon
Story photography by Mike Houska
Special thanks to Jim and Loryn Cummins

ISBN: 0-8499-5746-X

Printed and bound in Belgium

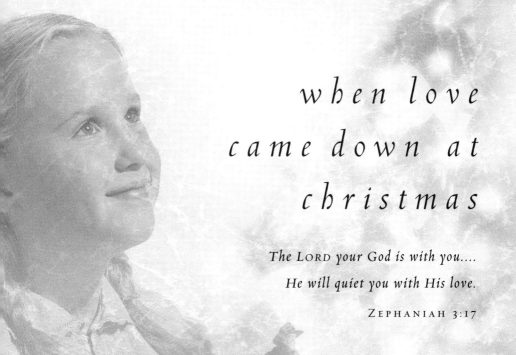

when love came down at christmas

The LORD your God is with you....

He will quiet you with His love.

ZEPHANIAH 3:17

IF ANYONE NEEDED A MERRY CHRISTMAS that year it was Dana. But the chances of that were slim. Eight years ago, on the day she was born, Daddy had left her and Mama and not even the remotest cousins knew where to forward his mail any longer—nor did they care. Then Mama had left just two weeks ago. But everyone knew what her forwarding address was for sure: *heaven*. After that, Mama's friend Miss Milly had put Dana on a plane for a place called Kansas City and between tears and hugs and kisses had promised to write.

The little girl's flight arrived early in the morning. She was groggy with sleep when the flight attendant woke her and tried to help her shoulder a pink and green backpack. But standing tall in all of her four-foot dignity she shook off the hovering hands and put it on herself.

I don't need help, she thought. *I'm eight years old and on my own. I can take care of myself just fine.*

Two stubby blonde braids and patches of stray hair stuck out wildly beneath her blue cloche hat. She looked exactly like a sorry little scarecrow, freed from its poles to sag all alone in a cornfield. Trudging out of the plane with the other somber passengers, she kept her eyes trained on the wheels of a suitcase in front of her. One wheel, which was off a bit, made a whirring noise like a tiny, toy helicopter. *I wish I could fly up to heaven right now and see Mama,* she thought to herself.

The gate area was stunningly bright, with a hundred rays of morning light reflecting off the glass. Dana shaded her eyes and almost walked past the special service attendant who was supposed to hand her and the documents over to her grandfather.

The two of them sat down and waited and waited, but there was no sign of him. Families around them squealed with delight and laughter. She watched them hug and kiss and slap one another on the back. The attendant tried to be friendly but Dana ignored her, searching beyond the smiling faces for a thatch of gray hair.

"Are you sure your grandpa knew when to meet you?" the attendant asked, pacing back and forth now in front of Dana's chair.

"Yes, he knew. Miss Milly said he'd be here. She's Mama's friend."

"We've been waiting twenty minutes. Where could he be?"

"I don't know."

"Let's go on down to baggage claim. He'll just have to find us there. I've got to meet another flight in ten minutes."

Even as the suitcases tumbled onto the baggage carousel Dana kept peering around bodies and over heads for the face in the photo on Mama's desk. When the crowd dispersed, just her two bags were left going round and round and round until a porter finally lifted them off.

"Are these your bags, little miss?" he asked in a jaunty voice.

She swallowed hard and nodded.

"Shame to let your bags spin round like that. They might get dizzy." He winked with a grin, lay the bags beside her, and walked off.

The attendant sat with her legs crossed and bounced one up and down while tapping the arm of the chair impatiently with long, red fingernails. She sighed and looked at her watch.

"Where can he be?" She was starting to sound angry.

Dana sat down on one of her bags and swallowed hard. *Don't cry*, she scolded herself fiercely. *Don't be a baby.* She put her head down and pushed her knuckles into her eyes to hold back the tears. Just then she felt a heavy hand on her head and heard a soft grunt.

"Sorry I'm late. Took me an hour and half to get here. The rain and sleet's got traffic backed up for miles . . . and the Christmas shoppers only add to the confusion."

"Well, better late than never." The attendant chattered with relief. She handed Grandpa the papers to sign and took off running for the escalators.

Dana looked up to a creamy grizzled beard that nearly hid a strong wrinkled face just the color of gingerbread. He flashed a quick smile, then promptly buried it back in the beard. Dana hopped up and grabbed her backpack.

By now she was no longer scared or embarrassed, she was just plain mad. "You're late!"

"I know. I just said I was. Also said I'm sorry. Are these two bags all your stuff, little girlie?"

Dana nodded and followed him out into the cold morning air. He was wearing a crisp black cowboy hat that had two little pins on it. One said

"Kansas" inset in a shape of the state. The other said, "Jesus Loves You." The letters were red and white. She craned her neck to read them.

He was a short, burly man, and she noticed he walked with a limp, which gave her a peculiar feeling cause she wasn't expecting it. Mama had never talked about him much, and you couldn't tell that sort of thing from a photo. *I wish he wouldn't call me "little girlie,"* she thought to herself. *I'm NOT little!*

THEY HEADED OUT TO THE BARREN, snow-gray parking lot, Dana scrambling to keep up with the rapid, uneven gait of his boots. Grandfather walked to a red truck, snapped down the back, and stacked the suitcases neatly inside. When he opened the door and tried to help her into the cab she shook him off. She didn't need help from him or anybody else. He looked at her, puzzled for a moment, then thought to himself. *We're not getting off to a very good start. Well, she's tired and hurting, like a little doe that's been pawed by a mountain lion. I'll have to give her time . . . If things don't work out . . . Pastor Ben said they'd have room for her at the Youth Ranch in Cottonport . . . but I do admire her gumption.*

Dana spent the trip purposefully looking out the window away from Grandfather while the suburbs gave way to country towns, and four-lane roads turned to muddy, farm tracks. He made small talk for a while but got tired of the one-way conversation and turned instead to the safe, familiar world of his own thoughts. *What kind of mess have I got myself into this time? I'm all she's got left in this world but that's no bargain. And how can an old rancher like me take care of a young girl from the city, anyway? I'm afraid this is going to be a very long, cold winter...whether we get more snow or not!*

At last they turned in past a John Deere tractor mailbox down a long gravel drive. The truck lurched over bumps and holes and slid to a stop in front of the house—an old country house with a broad front porch. It was white, bleached from all the years of laying in the sun at the end of the drive like a cat with a flattened tail, gazing through half-shut eyes at the woods nearby. Nestled at its back was a small, red barn, and on its western side, in front of the barn, lay a large fenced pasture. As Dana slid out of the truck, something caught her eye. She looked back quickly and sucked in her breath. At the far end of the field a black mare, tall and stately, was galloping in wide

circles. Her legs were slim and strong and her coat gleamed in the bright rays of sun breaking through the clouds.

Grandfather turned in surprise to see Dana staring at the horse. "That's Rhiannon," he explained eagerly. "She's a good horse. Used to be your grandmother Rosie's. Your mother loved to ride her, too, . . . before she moved to the city . . . and got married . . ." His voice trailed off.

They watched the horse for a moment, both lost in thought. Grandfather rested his eyes on the little girl at his side. *She's such a tiny little thing, but full of spunk. Just like her mother at that age. I'll bet she loves horses like her mama did too.* The puckered frown had slid off her face for one brief moment, and there was a spark of light in her sad green eyes.

He shook himself out of the reverie. "Let's go inside and get something to eat."

THE BROAD, SQUARE LIVING ROOM was unkempt but clean. Dana slouched on the edge of a blue checkered armchair and clicked the remote button between three equally blurry television stations, while Grandfather clanged pots and pans in the kitchen. He hummed one tune over and over again and every time he came to the same spot, he sang out in a loud bass voice, "His truth goes marching on!" then went back to humming again. Over the smell of fried hamburgers she thought how strange it seemed not to hear Mama singing in the kitchen. But she didn't dare think about that.

"Come and eat," Grandfather called out. "The food's ready."

Dana toyed with the idea of stubbornly refusing to eat, but her stomach rumbled in protest. She walked into the kitchen where Grandfather was pouring ketchup onto a hamburger bun, and for the first time, noticed that his hands were shaking. The red plastic bottle zigzagged all over the place.

She picked up the top bun and examined the hamburger critically. "I hate mustard! And onions . . . and pickles . . . and relish!"

Grandfather looked affronted. "What do you eat? Just bread and meat?"

"I like ketchup. That's all."

Grandfather grunted, took the only patty left, and slapped it onto a bun. "There you go. Fix it yourself."

While Dana nibbled at the hamburger she kept her eyes glued to the chipped, blue-willow plate in front of her. Grandfather rested his elbows on the old pine table warmed through the years to the color of golden honey.

"I know this isn't the way you and me wanted it. We've both had too many sad times, but I hope we can make the best of it." He sighed. "School's out for the Christmas break. That'll give you time to get settled before classes start in January."

Dana didn't look up and didn't reply. She had forgotten all about Christmas. *But what did it matter? Without Mama there could be no Christmas.* And she didn't dare think about that or the tears would start running down her cheeks. She vowed that Grandfather would never see her cry. She would never let him, or anyone, know how much she hurt. They didn't need to know about that.

She took a drink of the slightly soured orange juice and bit into the dry

hamburger. Grandfather started to say something, but changed his mind. So they sat in silence and munched, two weary survivors thrown onto the raft of life together through no choice of their own.

When she got up to leave the table he explained that her bedroom would be the one next to the bathroom at the end of the hall. He carried her bags into the room, set them down gingerly, and turned to leave. "If you need anything, just let me know."

Dana closed the door, fell onto the bed, and was relieved to be able to cry at last.

She cried because Mama was gone and here she was living in a forsaken, dreary house with an old man who was supposed to be her grandfather but who was, in truth, a complete stranger.

She cried because she missed her school and her friends. She missed the cozy apartment Mama had fixed up snug as a rabbit's burrow. And she missed Miss Milly, too. Everyone she cared about was gone. She would never see them again . . . she would never go home . . . she was all alone.

And so she cried some more.

WHEN DANA WOKE THE NEXT MORNING there was a chill in the air, but she was warm under a thick faded quilt someone had thrown over her in the night. Padding quietly down the hall, she found Grandfather rocking back and forth in front of a roaring fire, a large black Bible balanced on one of his knees.

"Oh, hello." He smiled. "There's cereal on the counter. I didn't know which kind you liked, so I bought several." His eyes dipped back into the book.

After breakfast, he said he had some chores to take care of in town. "Feel free to wander about outside, but don't go into the woods. They're full of chiggers and ticks, and it's easy to get lost. Maybe this afternoon we can drive into town and visit the library. You might be able to find something to keep your mind off of . . . out of trouble."

He smiled tentatively and limped across the room in an uneven gait. Pushing the black cowboy hat down on the back of his head, he waved good-bye and closed the back door with a bang.

Dana sat on the sagging couch, miffed that Grandfather would just walk out and leave her alone. He hadn't even invited her along. *Well*, she

Christmas Eve, 2 am
        Heavy snow is falling down
                and the streets, clothed in white
echo songs that were sung by candlelight

when love came down

We're alive and we can breathe
        but do we really care for this world in need?
        There's a choice we must make each and every day

So close your eyes and share the dream
                Let everyone on earth believe
        The child was born, the stars shone bright
and love came down at Christmas time
                and love came down at Christmas time

Christmas Eve, 2 am
Heavy snow is falling down
and the streets, clothed in white
echo songs that were sung by candlelight

when love came down

We're alive and we can breathe
but do we really care for this world in need?
There's a choice we must make each and every day

So close your eyes and share the dream
Let everyone on earth believe
The child was born, the stars shone bright
and love came down at Christmas time
and love came down at Christmas time

thought, *I don't care anyway. I'd rather be by myself. What's there to be scared of way out here in the middle of nowhere? Besides, I'm old enough to take care of myself. I don't need him or anybody . . . And I'll go into the woods if I want to. He's not my boss.*

She decided not to unpack her suitcases; she wanted things left just like they were. After changing into a pair of jeans and a bright red sweater she wandered outside. The quiet startled her. There was hardly a sound to be heard at all. It was like Mama's vacuum had come and sucked up the constant clashing of honking horns and screeching tires from the streets of the city and left a soft, quiet hush that felt like a hug from Miss Milly. It made you feel good inside, and safe.

Dana walked towards the pasture, drawn like a moth to a lamp. Rhiannon was standing calm, straining and stretching her neck to reach a patch of tall fescue at the edge of the fence. Dana tore up a clump of the grass, climbed to the second rung of the wooden fence, and held it out gingerly. Rhiannon ambled forward, nodded to the girl as if in greeting, and promptly began munching the stalks in her hand.

When Dana patted the horse's head cautiously, it felt warm and smooth. She wondered what it would be like to ride across the fields on the animal's sturdy back and thought of the time last year when Mama had said she could stick her head out the window of the train for just a minute. The wind had torn the hat off her head, and she had laughed at the wind showing off like that, so sure of itself. Is that what it would be like? To ride across the fields forever? *I wish we could run far away and find my daddy.*

THE TWO WERE TOGETHER AGAIN in the late afternoon when Grandfather roared up the drive, honking and waving out the window. Dana tried to ignore him but he kept tooting the horn. Finally, she stuck her hands deep into her pockets and wandered over to the edge of the drive. He was taking the ropes off a lush pine tree strapped to the back of the truck, and when she came into view he grinned and called out, "It's a Christmas tree! Ain't it a beauty?"

Dana rolled her eyes and walked toward the house. *What a silly old man! Doesn't he understand? I don't want to have any Christmas. Not without Mama!* She ignored his struggles to drag the tree up the front steps and across the wide

porch to the living room, even when she heard him wheezing and saw him rub his hip and grimace in pain. She sat at the window with her back to him. She was staring at the forest . . . thinking.

Grandfather set the tree up in the corner of the living room and clambered about the house searching for the Christmas decorations. He hadn't touched them since Grandma Rosie died three years ago. He hadn't had the heart. It would only have stirred up painful memories, and what was the point? Christmas was about loving and caring and giving and you couldn't do much of that when you lived all alone. Sure, he was glad to help out at the church and the folks there were especially kind to him this time of the year, but it just wasn't the same without your own kin. He had thought this year might be different, might be a tiny bit joyful. But things weren't looking too good.

He finally found the boxes marked "Christmas keepsakes" up in the attic and carried them down to the tree. He went into the kitchen to wash off the sap and dust from his hands and called out to Dana.

"Wanna help me decorate the tree?"

"No!"

There was a pause and Grandfather spoke again, more insistent. "Why mope around? I could use your help. Besides, I brought a large pizza from town and we can't eat 'til the tree's decorated."

Suddenly, Dana realized she hadn't eaten anything since early that morning. She groaned loudly, just to get her point across, and shuffled over to the tree.

"You do the bottom part. I'll do the top." Grandfather said. "Tell you what. I'll put the pizza on this little table so we can grab a bite while we work. I don't know about you, but I'm starving!"

In spite of the pepperoni pizza, Dana resolutely set out to do a poor job on the tree. What did she care? It wasn't her tree and these weren't her ornaments. They were silly little things—angels, glittering stars, cotton-ball sheep—not nearly as nice as the painted balls Mama had made for their tree. But Grandfather encouraged her every effort and praised her even when she obviously did a poor job.

When all of the ornaments were on the tree, he placed a six-inch star at the top, making sure it was ramrod straight, set at an exact, military balance.

Then he sat back and admired the tree . . . but Dana didn't want to look at it.

It only reminded her of last year's Christmas, when she and Mama had filled their perfect little tree to brimming with popcorn and balls and lights. Mama was fanatical about Christmas. Every year she set out the decorations on Thanksgiving and put them away with great reluctance in late January. She played Christmas songs over and over until they no longer seemed like individual songs, but melded together into one sweet sound of the season. She baked cookies and candy for weeks and gave them in baskets to each neighbor in the building. Then on Christmas day she and Miss Milly chopped celery and onion and gizzards and made a feast of turkey and dressing for their little group of friends. Mama always tried hard to make it a day of joy and laughter.

Dana closed her eyes hard to squeeze out the memories but the lump in her throat kept growing till she thought she would choke. She threw down a tattered angel and ran to her room.

Grandfather stood beside the tree and shook his head. Pain was a lonely experience. But sometimes, climbing out of the pain required a push. He took a step to go after her and nearly stumbled over an oblong box protruding beneath the wing chair. He picked it up and found inside the delicate porcelain crèche Rosie used to set out each year. He could still hear her clear voice. "I'm going to send the crèche to Margaret, come the first of the year. She'll take good care of it and give it to Dana some day." But Rosie never did send it. And now she was gone and Margaret was gone. There was no one left but Dana and him. Nothing left but the hurting . . . and the pain . . .

His callused finger traced the delicate blue figure of Mary holding the Christ child in her arms. He thought how she, too, had suffered pain and hurt. And how Joseph had suffered. Just think of the humiliation, confusion, and misunderstandings. Yet there was a great love there, too. *Funny,* he thought, *how the love and the suffering were all tied up together. How the love could ease the pain of the suffering. But pain without love? Well, that could drive a person to . . .*

DANA AWOKE IN THE MIDDLE OF THE NIGHT crying and trembling with fear. Forgetting where she was, she screamed in the darkness again and again. Grandfather threw open the door and flipped on the light. A tattered gray sweat-suit flopped loose over his ankles and elbows, and his hair stuck out from his head every which way like a halo meant for Scrooge's Angel of Christmas Past.

"What's wrong? What's wrong?"

He moved toward the bed but Dana covered her face with the blanket. Suddenly she remembered where she was and why she was there. Her voice was muffled. "Nothing's wrong. I . . . I . . . just . . . had a bad dream."

Grandfather stood with his arms hanging limp, pondering what to do next. "Must've been the pizza. I don't much care for the stuff they make in town. Not fresh, like your grandma used to make. Now *that* was pizza." His voice trailed off as Dana deliberately turned her back to him and pulled the blankets up over her head.

She heard the uneven shuffle of his feet as he limped down the hall and felt a twinge of regret. *Why am I so mean to him?* She wondered. *I just don't like*

him. He can't cook, and he walks funny. And I don't care about him anyway. Deliberately tucking the blankets under her chin, she quickly fell asleep.

THE NEXT MORNING SHE FOUND A NOTE on the kitchen table. "Lunchmeat + cheese in fridge. Bread on table. Back 2nite."

Dana wasn't bothered about being alone. She was used to that—but she wasn't used to being bored. At home there had been shelves of books to read, a wide selection of television stations, video games, telephone calls with her friends from school . . . What would she do all day here? Grandfather had said she could look through his collection of National Geographics, but that was about as exciting as tapioca pudding. She ran to the pasture to feed Rhiannon, but the mare was only a faint black shape at the far end of the field.

Warming her hands inside the pockets of her blue parka, Dana wandered down the drive, scuffing her shoes along the gravel. Suddenly the woods that spread along the western side of the house caught her attention, and a curious thought crept into her mind. *I wonder what's in that forest? I could go exploring. I might find something really cool!*

She ran to the kitchen and threw together some ham and cheese sandwiches then placed them in a grocery sack she found under the sink. Humming to herself, she closed the back door and walked to the edge of the woods. Right in plain view, an overgrown path ran parallel to the trees. When it dipped into a shaded glen, she hesitated a moment but defiantly shrugged her shoulders and marched on. *That old man's not my boss. I can do what I want!*

Though it wasn't long before the path petered out, Dana forged ahead, deciding it was more adventuresome to explore without a path anyway. All too soon she realize that the woods she had been in before were nothing like this. She was used to city-park forests of evenly spaced trees and smooth, sun-washed paths free of brush and stray growth. The trees in this forest grew riotous and packed in. They were choked with sticker bushes and brambles. They didn't soar high overhead; they grew low, as if to keep a suspicious eye on their neighbors.

Dana trudged farther into the forest, crying out in pain when thorns cut into her fingers and face. A sharp branch tore a wide gap in her pants and left a long scratch down the side of her leg. She considered turning back, but stubbornly hiked on. Every now and then, in rapid bursts of noise, birds squawked in the trees overhead.

Eventually she found a huge cedar tree and sat wearily at its base. Her shoes were caked with mud, her pants speckled with dirt and blood. She pulled a sandwich out of the sack only to find it too soggy and dirty to eat, so she threw it on the ground and sat defiantly with her chin in her hands, resting her elbows on her knees. The leaves and broken twigs sticking out of her hair at odd angles gave her the appearance of a rebellious woodland nymph.

She leaned against the trunk of the tree and listened to the breeze whoosh through the branches above.

Gradually, without warning, the sun dipped over the horizon and left nothing but a dusky light fading fast from the sky. The night air began its habitual slide toward freezing. Dana sat up in panic and dashed headlong into the brambles desperate to find her way back to the house. She ran and fell and pushed her way through the forest searching through the growing darkness for a light . . . any light to guide her out of the forest . . . to guide her home.

By now she knew she was lost and freezing cold. Wild, frightening thoughts darted through her mind. *Grandfather won't know where I am. He'll never find me . . . I'll die out here . . . A wild animal will attack me . . . That'll serve the old man right for leaving me alone. . . .* Her body shook and her teeth chattered as she huddled at the base of a tree.

She started to cry.

Suddenly, out of the darkness, faint and far away, someone called her name, "Dana . . . Dana . . . where are you?"

She jumped up and screamed over and over. "I'm here. Over here! Grandpa, I'm here!"

It wasn't long before Grandfather came crashing through the woods, a lantern in one hand and a wide, long knife in the other. His heart melted at the sight of her tear-stained face, her muddy clothes and matted hair. When he wrapped his coat around her and held her tight she sobbed quietly. He had wanted to punish her, to unleash his anger on her. He had meant to be tough on her, but she touched a soft spot in his heart that turned him to mush.

"Let's get back home, little girlie. It's getting ready to snow."

DANA SLEPT LATE THE NEXT MORNING, exhausted from last night's trauma. She and Grandfather had walked through the forest with snow falling thicker and faster by the minute. It had been a long walk . . . nearly five miles, he had said with amazement. Once home he ordered her to soak in a tub of hot water for a good twenty minutes "to kill the ticks." She had never been so glad to put on her favorite wool pajamas. Grandfather got out some antiseptic cremes and bandages to clean her cuts and scratches. While he worked gently to ease her pain she noticed the ugly cuts and bruises covering his hands and face. He'd gotten hurt in the woods, too. But he never said a word about it. He'd gotten hurt trying to find her.

After a plate of scrambled eggs and a mug of steaming hot chocolate, he said she'd better get to bed or she would catch pneumonia. As she drifted off to sleep she thought he would probably punish her in the morning, and she wondered what he would do.

She'd have to face that tomorrow.

IT WAS THE BRIGHT GLEAM IN THE ROOM that woke her. The bed and the dresser and the walls all radiated with a sparkling florescence. She ran to the window and saw that the storm had colored everything in the night—the world was snow white. She grabbed on her robe, ran down the hall, and found Grandfather rocking by the fire. He looked tired, more tired than she had ever seen him. He was reading his Bible, as usual, and every so often shook his head to himself.

Suddenly, he looked up and saw her standing sheepishly in the doorway. "Get your clothes on and go to the barn. I'll be waiting for you out there."

It felt like a rock had fallen to the pit of her stomach. He was going to beat her. He would punish her for going into the woods. Then he'd probably send her away . . . to an orphanage or some other horrible place. And she deserved it.

Tears pricked her eyes as she changed into her jeans and shirt. *Good thing I didn't unpack my suitcase. I wish I could just disappear so no one would ever have to be bothered with me again.*

She put on her coat and an old pair of boots abandoned by the back door. The freezing air stung her face as she clomped over the snow to the barn and through the open door. Grandfather was standing by a bale of hay.

"Come here, Dana."

She lowered her head and walked obediently to his side. When he raised his hand, she cringed, waiting for the blow.

But rather than pain, she felt his hand soft on her shoulder.

"I was scared outta' my wits when I came home yesterday and you were gone. My heart nearly busted in two. Hearing you answer my call in the forest was one of the most wonderful sounds I've ever heard."

Dana didn't know what to say. He had caught her off guard. She was confused. Wasn't sure she heard what he said. "I'm . . . I'm . . . sorry about the forest, Grandpa. I'm really sorry."

Grandfather nodded. "Listen, would you rather move away from here? I'd like for you to stay. You're all I've got left in the world. But I know it ain't easy living with an old man. If you'd rather be with other kids, I could probably get you a spot down at the Youth Ranch."

She stood still for a long while, thinking about what he had said. Then she thought about last night and the way he had held her hand tight in the snowstorm. Surely he must have felt the bitter cold, but he kept her wrapped in his coat. And no matter how bad his leg hurt he kept walking hour after hour to find her and bring her home.

Gently she shook her head. "I'd like to stay, if I may." Her voice was small and quiet.

"Good!" Grandfather's face beamed with a broad smile. "Because I didn't know how I was gonna ship your Christmas present to you."

"Christmas?" Dana had completely forgotten it was Christmas morning. She looked around bewildered. There were no packages here. What was he talking about?

"Come with me." Grandfather took her hand and led her to the far side of the barn, where Rhiannon was contentedly chewing a mouthful of hay. There beside her . . . lay a bright-eyed, black colt. Dana gasped.

"What a beautiful little colt!"

"He sure is. And he's all yours! Rhiannon and I were up most of the night making sure he got here on time."

She stood in awe, dumb-founded. "You did this for me?"

Tears ran in tiny rivulets down her cheeks. "But I don't deserve it."

Grandfather put his arm around her shoulders. "Sometimes, what we need the most is what we deserve the least. In fact, that's exactly why love came down at Christmas."

CHRISTMAS MEMORIES

So Merry Christmas everyone
                    and peace throughout the year
           the time has come to celebrate
                    so let your voices fill the air
Everyone, watch and pray
                    that the sun will shine on a brighter day
           Join your hands, lift them high
                              for this gift of life

when love came down at Christmas time

So close your eyes and share the dream
                    Let everyone on earth believe
           The child was born, the stars shone bright
                    and love came down at Christmas time
                    and love came down at Christmas time

So Merry Christmas everyone
and peace throughout the year
the time has come to celebrate
so let your voices fill the air
Everyone, watch and pray
that the sun will shine on a brighter day
Join your hands, lift them high
for this gift of life

when love came down at Christmas time

So close your eyes and share the dream
Let everyone on earth believe
The child was born, the stars shone bright
and love came down at Christmas time
and love came down at Christmas time

One of my favorite things about Christmas is the emphasis on tradition—as a family, we know we're going to do many of the same things every year, and we love it! For instance, at some point in our celebration, we know we're going to read the Christmas story from the Bible and pray together. It's just something we've always done, and will continue to do.

Another tradition established during my childhood in Oklahoma

was our annual Christmas tree search. The day after Thanksgiving, Mom, Dad, Misti (my younger sister) and I traveled all over the area, looking at various Christmas tree farms, searching for just the right tree to cut down, drag to the car, and haul home. Of course, we all had our opinions as to which was the best tree.

"I want this tall one!"

"No, I like that little one over there."

"Look, the branches on this one are much better for decorating."

The perfect tree was the one we all agreed on—usually a large, fat

tree. Mom loved those trees with wide, full branches. When we could finally agree, Dad sawed down the tree and we loaded it on top of the car or in a pickup truck if we happened to have one, drove home, and stood the tree up inside our house. We couldn't imagine having an artificial tree in our home. Our tree had to look, feel, and smell like the woods it came from.

Another highlight of the Christmas season was the annual visit to our grandparents in Munday, Texas, a small town of about sixteen hundred people. Both Mom's and Dad's family members got together to go Christmas caroling all over town. Since Munday was a close-knit community, when we approached the door of neighbors, everybody knew us. They turned on their porch lights or invited us to come inside for something to eat and to sing for them. Mostly, we just stood out in front of the homes and sang the old-time, favorite carols. The neighbors were always appreciative.

On Christmas Eve, our family gathered around the piano at home. Mom played the piano, and we sang and sang all our favorite Christmas songs. Singing together around the piano has always been one of the most special of our Christmas Eve traditions. On Christmas Eve, after all the last minute gift-wrapping, we'd gather as a family to read the Christmas story. Mom usually read the account from the gospel of Luke, and then Dad topped off the evening with a time of prayer.

Mom and Dad always emphasized that Christmas was not about getting gifts, but about the Giver, about God giving His Son to the world as the means of salvation. My sister and I knew from early childhood that Christmas was about the birth of Jesus, and that Santa Claus was simply a fun character. The real focus of our celebration was always Christ.

MOST UNUSUAL CHRISTMAS TREE

One Christmas, after Mom and Dad had retired and moved back to the farm in Munday, Texas, Dad decorated the outside of the house with all the usual colored lights. But to top it off, he found a huge Texas tumbleweed (nearly as big as car!), and placed it in the front yard. He decorated it with cotton and colored lights, making it a "Texas Christmas Tree."

FAVORITE CHRISTMAS FOOD

My sister's and my favorite Christmas food is our mom's broccoli and rice casserole. It may not be a typical Christmas dish, but we love it!

FAVORITE CHRISTMAS MUSIC

I love Nat King Cole's Christmas album. I've played it so much that I need a new one. Other favorite Christmas albums included Perry Como, and, of course, Bing Crosby. Nowadays, one of my favorites is Mariah Carey's Christmas album, 4-Him's great album of Christmas songs, and one of my husband's all time favorites: The Carpenters' Christmas album.

I first began to understand the true spirit of Christmas when I was about five years old. My dad had just gotten out of military service and, with the help of my mother, was trying to put himself through college. We were living in Jacksonville, Arkansas, in a small (but nice) mobile home, on one small income—a no-frills budget!

That Christmas season, I heard Mom and Dad say, "We're going to go down to the television station, and pick up a letter to Santa."

SHELLEY BREEN

"What's that?" I asked.

"Well, some parents don't have enough money to buy their children presents at Christmas time, so their children write a letter to Santa, and send it to the television station. Then other people, who are more fortunate, pick up a letter from a child and buy some presents to help make Christmas special for him. So that's what we're going to do."

Even as a child, the irony was not lost on me that we were as poor as dirt, yet Mom and Dad felt compelled to help other families. I'll always be grateful for their example of unselfish love. I still remember the pained look on my mom's face when she hung up from calling the mother of the child we were going to help. The little girl had quite a list—far more requests, for more expensive presents than my parents could afford to give. But Mom and Dad did the best they could to help. I'll never forget their giving when they had so little. That was one of the most significant Christmas seasons of my life, and it instilled "a giving spirit" in my heart and mind.

It was that same Christmas, when I first learned the truth of the adage: "As we give, we also receive." I admit that when I saw Mom and Dad buying presents for "less fortunate" kids, I was tempted to think, Hey! What about me? What kind of Christmas are we going to have if we give so much away? But when I walked out into the living room of our trailer, there, under the Christmas tree, was my first Barbie house. It was the one present I wanted more than any other, but I hadn't dared to dream that I might actually get it. It was a great lesson to learn: It's not how much you give, but it's about giving what you can; that as we give more we also receive more; and as we give to others, God gives back to us.

Our church in Little Rock, Arkansas had a candlelight service on Christmas Eve, and my family and I always attended, from the time I was a little girl. We went to church at 7:00 in the evening for our regular Christmas Eve service, then we returned home where Mom always had a big spread of food ready for us. Then at 11:00 P.M., we went back to church for a candlelight service. It was such a moving time when, at the conclusion of the service, right around midnight, everyone in the congregation lit their candles and sang, "Silent Night." I can still see the beautiful sight of those candles raised in the air, and hear the voices singing, "Christ the Savior is born!" It always brought the focus back to Jesus coming into this world as a human being—the Incarnation—and that's what Christmas is all about.

To this day, I look forward to going home at Christmas, because I know Mom is going to say, "There are some Hello Dollies in the refrigerator." If you've never tasted some Hello Dollies, you're missing one of life's great

treats! They are sort of a combination of graham crackers, butterscotch, and chocolate chips, nuts, and coconut with "sweet milk" over it. Mmmm-mmmm! They're really good!

FAVORITE CHRISTMAS MOVIE

Miracle on 34th Street (both the black and white version and the color version). I've watched it almost every year, since I was a little girl.

FAVORITE CHRISTMAS MUSIC

My grandpa died when I was about seven years old, and his favorite Christmas song was "Joy to the World." Ever since grandpa died, every time I hear that song it touches me in a special way. It reminds me of his faith in Christ as well as my own.

The Christmas season is my favorite time of year. I love it and always have! My family didn't have a firm tradition of attending church services on Christmas Eve, but we did have a tradition of attending the annual Christmas morning service at our church. Imagine waking up on Christmas morning, seeing all the wonderful presents under the tree, and

not being able to open them until after church! Knowing how excited we were, our parents allowed us to open one present on Christmas Eve, before going to bed. Mom and Dad honestly thought that we could go to sleep after opening one present. No way! We were way too excited by that time!

One Christmas, Mom took me to an apartment where a young, single mother lived with her children in absolute poverty. They had very little food, and their beds were mattresses thrown on the floor. We had gotten their name and learned a little about their circumstances from our church.

Mom and I went to the store and bought food for them to cook for Christmas dinner and special toys for the children. The single mother thanked us over and over. She was so grateful for any little thing that we gave to them, and the kids were so excited about their presents. Seeing the expressions on their faces is a Christmas memory I'll never forget. Not only did that experience help a needy family, it emphasized to me that although we certainly weren't wealthy, we had been blessed with so much and had a responsibility to share with others.

FAVORITE CHRISTMAS TRADITION

Our family started celebrating Christmas in November, observing the Advent calendar on the four Sundays of Advent before Christmas. We had an old wreath and four candles, and each Sunday we read a passage of Scripture about Christmas and lit one of the Advent candles. It was a great way to keep the focus of Christmas on Christ and to build our anticipation.

FAVORITE CHRISTMAS FOODS

Everyone laughs at me when I admit that my favorite Christmas treats are those little barbecued "smokies," those round smoked sausages, cooked in barbecue sauce in a crock pot. I love to have those at Christmas parties.

FAVORITE CHRISTMAS MUSIC

I love all the Christmas carols, but two of my favorites are "Away in a Manger" and "Silent Night."

As for Christmas albums, I love Elvis' Blue Christmas album. It's kind of cheesey but I love it. I also enjoy 4-Him's Christmas album.

FAVORITE CHRISTMAS MOVIE

My all-time favorite is *White Christmas,* because when I was a little girl I enjoyed musicals with the singing and dancing and the innocent romance that went into those kinds of productions. I still beg Stu to watch it with me every Christmas.

I have three sisters—Katie, Christie, and Angie—and when we were little girls, every Christmas we woke up before the sun was barely up and ran into our parents' bedroom. "Come on, Mom and Dad! We're ready to go downstairs!"

"Now, girls, go sit on the gold bench and wait until we get ready," one of our parents would say. My sisters and I reluctantly retreated to the gold bench at the top of our staircase. We sat there waiting anxiously . . . for what seemed like hours!

TERRY JONES

Finally, we'd hear Dad say, "Okay, girls. We'll be there in a minute." Mom and Dad took their time, got up, showered, and put on their clothes. Meanwhile, we girls were going bonkers! "Mom! Dad! Come on!"

Just when we thought we couldn't stand it another minute, Mom and Dad came out and we went downstairs and celebrated Christmas.

The mystery of Christmas is so precious to us. Just as Mom and Dad used to make us wait at the top of the stairs, today, my husband,

Chris, and I make our two-year-old son, Cole, wait, as well. We get the video camera ready and say, "Okay, Cole!"

He gets so excited, as does his baby brother Luke.

I want our sons, Cole and Luke, to know that God's greatest gift to us at Christmas was His Son, Jesus Christ. That's why we celebrate, because God loves us so much He gave His Son to come to earth and die for us. Jesus came to earth as a tiny baby, grew to be a man, and died for us. We don't ever want to miss the mystery or lose a sense of awe of who Jesus is and what He has done for us. Chris and I want our children to know that Christmas is not just about getting gifts, it's about giving—not just material things, but giving of yourself, giving memories, hugs, kisses, and love, just as God gave His Best for us.

FAVORITE CHRISTMAS TRADITION

Mom hung special Christmas stockings for each of us every Christmas. When we were younger, she filled the stockings with candy canes and popcorn balls, and other treats. Now that we are older, she still hangs the stockings, but now she fills them with small containers of makeup, lipstick, breath mints, and other "essentials." And she still includes a pair of socks for each of us.

FAVORITE CHRISTMAS FOODS

We have a huge Christmas dinner every year. Mom cooks up a fabulous turkey dinner, complete with sweet potatoes, corn, stuffing, and cranberry sauce. She also makes these wonderful peanut butter and chocolate cookies. Anything with chocolate makes me happy!

FAVORITE CHRISTMAS MUSIC

We lived near San Francisco when I was growing up, so each year at Christmas my family attended a performance of The Nutcracker, performed by the San Francisco Ballet. I think I saw it performed at least ten times as a child, and now as an adult, Chris and I have gone to see it twice.